Rob Versus The Entitled

Defeating The Aggressive, Offended, and Easily Triggered With A Little Common Sense & A Lot Of Sarcasm.

Rob Anspach

Rob Versus The Entitled
Defeating The Aggressive, Offended, and Easily Triggered With A Little Common Sense &
A Lot Of Sarcasm.

Copyright © 2021 Anspach Media
Cover design by: Freddy Solis

All rights reserved. No part of this book may be reproduced or transmitted in any form or by any means without written permission from the author.

ISBN 13: 978-1-7324682-7-6

Printed in USA

Disclaimer:
Oh yes, we must have a disclaimer…it makes the lawyers happy. The author has spent a lifetime using sarcasm as a means to grow his business. He shares interactions in this book that you may or may not agree with, his actions and communications are contrary to what most customer service gurus teach. But, it works for him and could work for you too, although highly doubtful.

What People Are Saying

"I always expect to like anything Rob Anspach writes. Rob is smart, bright, sharp and very funny/sarcastic. His latest effort, "Rob Versus The Entitled" is no exception. I learned and smiled from beginning to end . . . even laughing out loud several times. Get out your Hi-Liter pen and dig in! This one is a real keeper."
~ **Ben Gay III**, www.bfg3.com

"ROB... LOVED the book! Definitely worth the read! Made me chuckle more than once and I even have a few favorites. Thank you!"
~ **Faith Sage**

"I'm not usually one for sequels. Too often, they've wrecked franchises. But Rob is different. The scripts keep showing up on his doorstep...and they are gold. At this point, I'm pretty sure if Rob was asked "If you were stuck on a deserted island for 5 years, what would you bring with you?", he would reply: "A solar-powered cell-phone with Caller ID". By the time he got rescued, he'd have a half-dozen new books. This edition is my new favorite. I believe it should be combined with Mad Libs® and given to everyone over the age of 65 as a weapon against scammers. If my Dad was still alive, he would've gotten this book for Christmas."
~ **Steve Gamlin**

"Rob Versus the Entitled highlights a subject that makes people angry but does it in a way that you actually laugh instead. With each story, Rob addresses telemarketers and scam artists in such a way that most of us, deep down, would love to have the gumption to do ourselves. He does so with such tact and wit that the scammers are revealed as the frauds that they are. Rob uses humor, and an excellent sense of sarcasm, that truly make this compilation of stories a funny exercise on revenge best served." ~ **Russell Hoffman**

"I thought I was going to sit down and read just a few chapters and then realized I was on page 75 of Rob Anspach's new book Rob Versus The Entitled. I just couldn't stop reading...and laughing. Rob's wit and sarcasm are the healing balm we all need against those annoying scam calls. Get a couple copies for your friends, I guarantee you will laugh." ~ **Brad Szollose**, Host of Awakened Nation®

"This book is definitely worth the read, his quick wit is a detriment to those that open themselves to a chance to experience it. Once you start reading you will not want to put it down. Definitely worth of being in the Rob versus series. Keep up the great work you are doing Rob. Your books always make me smile and brighten my day." ~ **David L. Brown**, www.BusinessPlanAnswerMan.com

"I was completely outraged, triggered, and offended by this book. I was going to call the author and complain, but I didn't want to end up in his next one."
~ **Steve Sipress**

"I had Adobe Acrobat read it to me. Pretty deadpan delivery. But, funny. I kept getting interrupted by PITA calls and had to pause it a lot. The chapter "So You Want to Be On My Podcast" was an almost word-for-word replica of two calls I sarcastically fielded a couple weeks back. The first was from an attorney publishing a book seeking an interview on our Personal Injury Primer podcast. The other from a car body repair service entrepreneur convinced that listeners to a personal injury-themed podcast would love hearing about a body repair shop. ... I don't carry a master sarcasm card like you, Rob, but my native skills coupled with the lessons learned from reading this book, I hope will get me a journeyman sarcasm card." ~ **David Holub** www.DavidHolubLaw.com

"The book is great. I love your humor."
~ **Christine Schlonski**, www.ChristineSchlonski.com

"As soon as I got a copy of Rob's book, I immediately sent it to my daughter. The next day, we sat at the kitchen table reading the stories to each other, laughing at how Rob was able to confuse and waste the time of these annoying callers. We loved how he made heroic efforts to give back to these scammers exactly what they've been taking from the general public for so many years; our time and money. We found it hysterical that they didn't understand his movie references and clearly didn't get his sarcasm that so quickly cut to the quick their efforts to scam him out of his money. What makes Rob's books so funny and amusing is that each of us can relate to what he's going through. Why? Because we've all been in his situation. The only difference is that he's taken his wit and sarcasm to a whole new level that prompts you to laugh out loud and smile on the inside. By the time you finish reading each of his stories, you begin to wish that it was you who thought of these witty responses and comebacks that he so eloquently reproduces for us in his remarkable books. My daughter and I bookmarked various responses to use the next time one of these call centers call us asking us to press #1 asking for our information; whether it's from the IRS, the Sheriff's office, the warranty center or anyone looking to waste our time. We loved the latest book and highly encourage you to get your copy now." ~ **Gerry Oginski** www. Oginski-Law.com

"In a culture which is more and more entitled and prone to butt-hurt with every passing second, Rob Anspach is one aspirational SOB. Rob skewers the cancerous tumor of inflated egos, crybabies, and narcissism with a set of extraordinary sharp and sarcastic fangs. I can only aspire to be as sarcastic, biting, or funny as Rob is. Reading "Rob vs the Entitled" gave me a sense of satisfaction that someone, somewhere, is working to waste the time of the scammers, and working against the flood of people who feel that it's perfectly reasonable to take our time away without our permission. Rob, maybe someday I can grow up to be as cutting and intolerant as you are. I can only hope."
~ **Eric Ridley**, Estate Planning Attorney, www.RidleyLawOffices.com

"The Quadra-tome Of Sarcastic Engagement: Rob has pigeonholed just about every segment of society with his series of 'Rob Versus' books. His latest output collects a variety of true wit as he relates the daily contacts and requests that he receives. Not only does Rob put scammers on the defensive and they end up losing their cool due to their own bungling, but he adds terrific advice at the end of each segment so you can learn how to deal with the daily interruptions and annoyances in Rob's style. I heartily recommend this not only for the laughs, but the tips you'll glean from it." ~ **Paul Klein**

"Sarcasm is my native tongue and a true art form, but nobody skewers the perpetually entitled (and offended) like Rob does in this most recent masterpiece! This book demonstrates not only that the entitled among us are growing more and more bold, but that they can be defeated and demoralized with a little common sense and a heavy dose of the sarcastic arts. If sarcasm were a religion, Rob Anspach would be our High Priest. Well done!"
~ **Michelle Woolard Pippin** www.WomenWhoWow.com

"Dr. Sarcasm or: How I learned to defeat the easily triggered and love my inner jerk. Have you ever been so irritated by the calls from telemarketers, the comments, posts and messages from online associates easily triggered, offended and aggressive who believe they know better than you but you just don't know how you should respond or if you even should? Let Rob Anspach be your guide in navigating the sea of snowflakes. In his fourth installment in the Rob Versus series you'll enjoy more of his no BS attitude as he goes up against all the time suckers and turns the tide from a negative to a positive...for us the reader. You'll learn It's fun being a jerk in self-defense. You'll discover that the real jerks are the entitled robbing us of common sense, courtesy, time and money. Rob's got your back, he may not be the hero we think we need but he is the sarcastic hero we deserve to combat this mad, mad, mad world we live in and throat punch the insanity we endure. While the entitled get madder you'll be happier knowing you don't have to take their crap willingly anymore."
~ ***Erik Olson,*** Safe N Soft Carpet Cleaning www.CarpetCleaningBoise.com

"Rob Versus The Entitled is absolutely hilarious and a welcome respite from all the nonsense out in the world today. If you own your own business and find yourself constantly being interrupted by time wasters, this is a must read."
~**Tracy Kay**, Tracy Kay Consulting www.SalesReinvention.club

"Hey Rob, I really enjoyed your book! I don't usually answer the phone when I see that it's a solicitor or potential scammer calling, but after reading your book I have to admit that I've got a little FOMO, thinking about all the fun I'm missing out on. Not sure that I'll change my ways when it comes to accepting phone calls, but you've definitely inspired me to have a little more fun with the engagement I get from folks on social media. Thanks for the great laughs Rob!"
~ **Kevin Thompson**, Tribe For Leaders www.TribeForLeaders.com

"Can Sarcasm Change The Weather? I read this book in one sitting, nestled in my Sonoran Desert Arizona home. The absence of frigid winter weather tops my list of reasons why I love living here. Yet, "Rob vs. the Entitled" reminded me of how often, even here...in the desert...I encounter snowflake flurries. But not snowflakes that fall from the sky; these fall apart mentally and emotionally when something offends their delicate sensibilities. In society's quest to function better with each other, we have allowed our sensitivity to spiral out of control. People starve for truth while simultaneously walking on eggshells. If a product name, logo, or mascot offends someone, we execute it. Comedians have an ever-shrinking list of things they can make jokes about, and our leaders pander to the whims of a cancel culture who deceitfully fancy themselves as moral guardians. This book offers you a chance to stop taking yourself so darn seriously. It's a chance to laugh out loud at the absolute cluelessness of people, business practices, and scammers. It's also Bootcamp for every snowflake regardless of where they are on the political, ethnic, religious, or social scales (and yeah, there are snowflakes on all sides, so shut up). If you are easily hurt or offended by others' statements or actions, this book just might increase your weekly tissue budget. It's also filled with laugh-out-loud stories, life lessons and serves as a field manual for keeping your cool while fending off the inevitable encounter with a time-wasting fool." ~ **Tony Policci** www.TheCopyAvengers.com

"Got to page 45 drinking my coffee yesterday morning. Chuckles and full belly laughs. Also, solid knowledge bombs. I'm loving it so far."
~**Jen Grosso**, Bold Fire Institute www.boldfireinstitute.com

"I have finished reading Rob Anspach's latest book, "Rob Vs The Entitled," and of all the Rob versus books, this one certainly triggered me the most. Triggered howling fits of laughter that terrified my dogs and made my cats hiss at me. I completely disrupted their peaceful daytime routine with guffaws and thigh slaps. So if you are needing a quiet humorless environment without raucous joviality, don't buy this book. It will make you laugh way too hard."
~ **Paul Douglas**, Titan Marketing Solutions www.TitanMarketingSolutions.com

"As a business owner myself for 32 years, Rob mutually understands and is clearly a voice for us when trying to grasp the lack of common sense that is rampant in today's world of commerce : Rob's book is spot on and is an enjoyable read. Here's to the business owners like myself that endure and trudge on!"
~ **Monica Forte**, Making Magical Vacations Travel www.mmvacationstravel.com

"Interspersed in the lines of sarcastic wit are true gems of how to connect in business in an authentic way, how to handle fake leads intended to scam you, and how poorly conceived approaches are likely to be received. As part of *that family* in Tacoma, Washington, even my middle schoolers are gaining valuable insight into the business world. What would we do without Rob and the hilarity his insight brings? We don't want to know. Well done once again, Rob. Me and my family can hardly wait for the next book!" ~**Jocelyn Stewart** www.ucmj-defender.com

Table of Contents

Introduction.. 11
Chapter 1 - You Can't Afford Me!.. 13
    When They Want You But Can Not Afford You 14
    There's Always Another Choice.. 15
    Rude and Jerky.. 17
Chapter 2 - I Know You're Busy, But…..................................... 19
    How Can I Help You 20
    So You Want To Be On My Podcast... 22
    Third Time Is NOT A Charm 24
Chapter 3 - Why Did You Reach Out?.. 25
    Just Say No To Side Hustles 26
    I'm The Team Leader 28
    Have Your Team Do That 30
    No, Get Out!.. 33
    We Only Hire Local 34
    Invite Declined 36
    No Decision Maker Here... 38
Chapter 4 - Working For Free!.. 39
    Not Registered With Amazon Alexa 40
    Virtual Nonsense... 42
    Zoom, Zoom 44
Chapter 5 - Wasn't Me.. 45
    Why Did You Delete My Comment 46
    Just Admit It 48
Chapter 6 - Easily Offended 49
    Apparently My Tone Was Awful 50

You Are A Business Of Some Sort Right 52
Your Coach Is An Idiot 54
I Failed His Personality Test 56
I Am Mean 59

Chapter 7 - Trying To Scam Me? 61

Pfft, Not Leo's Brother 62
This Is The IRS 64
Grab A Pen And Paper 65
Agent M The Health Insurance Scammer 67
Scammer Might Have Covid 69
State Of Confusion 71
I'm Not The Customer You Are Looking For 73
I Guess Fhloston Paradise Isn't An Option 75
It's A Fake Page 76

Chapter 8 - PITA's Everywhere 77

We Really Want You & Your Team To Help Us 78
I Don't Need It, But They Want Me To Have It 80
No More Apps 82
Hey A-Hole 84
Oh My Gawd 88

Chapter 9 - One Of Those People 89

I'm A Big Fat Jerk 90
One Less Friend 92
Open House Extortion 94
Not My Dentist 94

Chapter 10 - I'm Sorry, Not! 95

Apology Call Meets HWP 96
Another Apology Call 98

  Lose My Email 100
Chapter 11 - GoDaddy's Finest *101*
  Eric From GoDaddy 102
  Chantelle from GoDaddy 103
  Gary From GoDaddy 104
Chapter 12 - To Heck And Back *105*
  Why Would You Invite Me To Your House 106
  How May We Irritate You 107
Chapter 13 - You're In The Book Now *109*
  I'll Sue You 110
  Congrats You're In The Book 113
  The Price is Normal, You are Not 115
  He Went From Clubhouse Into A Book 118
About The Author *121*
About The Editors *122*
  Parthiv Shah 122
  Ashley Armstrong 122
  Amy Tiemeyer 122
  Faith Sage 123
  Scott Paton 123
  Jaime McCormick 124
  Kristin Babik 123
  Emily Letran 124
Resources *125*
And One For The Road *131*

If I had a nickel every time this happened...

I make a comment on someone's post. Based on my experience, mind you. And someone responds. And I knew by the way they phrased their comment they were baiting me. So I was careful with my wording.

Until...

They made a stupid nonsensical "but it's science" comment.
And then I had to correct them.

Oh yeah...and I felt a devious smile form on my face.
It was glorious.

Then they commented again.
Grr...and my blood started to boil.
How dare they?

Snappy comeback to make them cry.
Then they threatened to report me to Facebook.
A-holes.

Then I got blocked.

Introduction

Over the years, I've become a magnet for these types of interactions. And, those on the other end of the exchange get to experience the full range of my sarcasm. And if they are lucky, they are immortalized in my books. As if luck had anything to do with it.

But this is Book 4 of the Rob Versus series and you'd think by now people would avoid the very circumstances that got their friends into hot water with me. Yeah, you would think. As you will soon find out, that's just not the case. And, fortunately for you, the reader, sarcasm is a beautiful way to handle any and all circumstances.

Now, what I will say, and to bring you up to speed, I did invite a few past readers to critique and edit this book. You will find their information under "About The Editors". I did this because…well…how I do things is a bit contrary to how other entrepreneurs might react and I certainly don't want you thinking my way is the only way. I mean it is, and you will certainly find that out, but I want you to have an open mind, at least right now. Got it?

As with the prior Rob Versus books in dealing with my interactions with scammers, morons, lousy customer service, fraudsters, fools and time wasters, this book follows suit and continues on with even more shenanigans, tomfoolery and the occasional verbal judo. It's a fast paced, laugh-out-loud riot session followed by a short thought, note or life lesson.

My goal is to educate you on the ways of entrepreneurship through entertainment. And sharing my adventures with you, even if they are triggering to some will, I hope, give you a better understanding of how to be a better entrepreneur.

It's not always easy.

There will be situations. Most likely screaming will be involved.

But if you use the lessons that I share in these books, you may even have something to write about in your own book, or in a future Rob Versus book. Hey, I'm counting on you, don't let me down. Study up. Learn my responses. Someday that power will come in handy. Trust me. Oh, and when it does, embrace it.

So without further ado…
And to get you on your way to learning sarcasm at its finest…

I give you, "Rob Versus The Entitled".

A book born from the effects the pandemic left on society. And one man's heroic effort to use common sense and sarcastic remarks to right the wrongs created by the easily offended, triggered, passive aggressive, self-anointed, overly righteous, scammy, phony, time wasting fools.

Enjoy the book

Rob Anspach

AnspachMedia.com

P.S. Adam's note below sums up everything about me…
"Rob Anspach has mastered the power of business education in a way few others can fathom. In his good-naturedly sarcastic way, he uses the power of storytelling to highlight best practices for business networking, marketing, and customer service excellence by highlighting real-world scenarios most people can relate to from their own day-to-day experiences. He subtly and subconsciously invites the reader to picture themselves in the situation, applying the tactics and strategies themselves, in a way that raises the bar for entrepreneurs and the companies they own and manage. This approach tends to imprint the lessons far more profoundly than through a whitepaper, or the latest "industry-shocking special report" - for this reason alone, join Rob in his crusade and gain from the experience!" ~**Adam Hommey**
Creator, The R.E.A.C.H. System www.TheReachSystem.com

Chapter 1

You Can't Afford Me!

"Not now, not ever…and I won't say "show me the money" because your money ain't worth the hassle."

When They Want You But Can Not Afford You

Hey Rob we would really like you to join our team.

Me: Join or Lead?

Them: Join, we already have a leader.

Me: And what would you pay me to Join your team?

Them: {tosses out a figure}

Me: Hmm, and what do you pay your leader?

Them: {hesitates...then tosses out a figure}

Me: Nah, I'll stay where I am... I pay myself more than you pay your leader.

Them: Would you reconsider?

Me: Sure, but it would require you to pay me triple what you are paying your leader.

Them: Oh, okay...so I guess we should keep looking.

Me: Or find a way to pay me.

{they hung up}

Note: Over the years I have been approached many times by people who think they can entice me to come work for them. The conversation usually ends the same as above. And, I've always turned them down. Maybe someday a company will offer me big bucks...but until then...all they'll get from me is...sarcasm.

There's Always Another Choice

Hey Rob, I really love what you are doing, can you give me a quote.
{message I received in my FB messenger}

Me: Sure, but first let's jump on a call so I can learn more about you.

Them: Does it have to be today?

Me: It doesn't have to be today, could be tomorrow, could be the next day, but if you want a quote I would think you need the help right away, correct?

Them: Yes, we need help figuring everything out, and also making new sales.

Me: Great let's get you scheduled.

{I schedule a time, potential client needs to reschedule, so I schedule a second time. Potential client keeps the new time slot and we talk for about 25 minutes. Wants the world, brags that money is no object - so I send a quote. Four days go by... then the chat messages continue.}

Them: Hey I got your quote of XXXX per month. Currently out of my ball park. What can you do for XXX per month?

Me: Not much.

Them: Can you be more specific?

Me: Okay, I can't do anything on the list of what I quoted.

Them: What? That doesn't make sense. Why give me a list if you can't do anything on it?

Me: Oh, I can do everything on the list for the quote I gave, just can't do any of it for what you wish to pay.

Them: Okay, what can you do for what I can afford?

Me: I can offer you a 45 minute phone consultation every month and review what you are doing and how to improve it.

Them: I don't want to do the digital marketing, that's your expertise.

Me: Yes, and I charge for my expertise.

Them: I can't afford you.

Me: Yes, we've established that.

Them: Now what?

Me: Either come up with the money for me to do what you need or pay me to consult you, your choice.

Them: Is there another choice?

Me: Sure.

Them: What is it?

Me: Contact someone else.

{and he blocked me}

Note: I've been told many times that I shouldn't treat people this way, that I should be more diplomatic in my approach, put my ego aside and legitimately help them. Nah, I like my way better. And frankly not only is it more entertaining but ultimately gets rid of people that are going to huge PITAs (pain in the asses).

Rude and Jerky

I commented in some group about social media.

I received about 50 likes to my comment...
and an employment proposal through chat.

So I reached out and said I'm not looking for a job as I'm very happy where I am.

Them: You sure, based on your comments you'd make a great social media manager.

Me: Oh yes, I like it where I am.

Them: What would it take for you to work with us?

Me: You can't afford me.

Them: Try me. We are open to suggestions.

Me: {gives offer}

Them: Wow, that is extremely high.

Me: Is it? Seems reasonable since I would need to be compensated for selling my media business and working for you.

Them: What, why didn't you say you owned your own business?

Me: One, you didn't ask. Two, you should have read my profile. And three, if you send employment proposals based on random comments then expect that some of the people responding to be agency owners.

Them: You don't have to be rude.

Me: Next time do some research before sending out employment proposals.

Them: I'm glad we didn't hire you, you seem to be a jerk.

Me: Exactly why I own my own business so when I get random employment proposals I can act rude and jerky...

...mission accomplished.

{and I was blocked}

Note: If you're one of those people who send out random employment offers and you just read the above interaction, I want you to take your hand and reach behind you and grab the back of your underwear and yank it straight up as hard as you can. Yeah, not fun is it? Well then, stop sending out random employment offers.

Chapter 2

I Know You're Busy, But…

"Oh yes, I love being interrupted by those who think I do nothing all day. As if I serve them, who'da thunk?"

How Can I Help You

Hey Rob, I know you're busy...

Me: Nah, I sit here all day waiting for you to contact me.

Them: Seriously?

Me: Oh yes, I've given up huge projects just so when the opportunity arises I'm here to help you.

Them: Wow, that's awesome.

Me: How can I help you?

Them: {pauses a bit} Do you really give up projects for me?

Me: Well let me ask you...were you considered Advanced Placement in school?

Them: No, but what's that have to do with anything?

Me: Well that's your answer.

Them: What's my answer?

Me: Dude, what do you need?

Them: I really don't think you wait for me all day, do you?

Me: What gave it away?

Them: F-You

Me: Yup, that's really what I was waiting for, that makes it all worth it.

Them: You wasted my time.

Me: Oh yes, it's my fault.

{and I got blocked}

Note: I know we live in a world that revolves around instant answers and "drop what you're doing and help me" attitude but honestly, can't I have some fun at the expense of others? Then write about it? Seriously, without these interactions millions of people around the globe would be denied the laughter they need to get through life. Did I say millions? I meant thousands. Okay, okay…it's one family in Tacoma Washington who have nothing better to do than to read my books every Friday night.

So You Want To Be On My Podcast

Hey Rob I would love to be on your podcast.

{message received in my FB chat}

Me: Cool, when.

Them: As soon as possible.

Me: Well, I record via Zoom and the video goes to YouTube the same day and the audio goes to about 25 podcast channels but right now there's about a 12-13 week delay in audio.

Them: That's ridiculous.

Me: What is?

Them: That you have such a delay.

Me: Again the video goes out right away so you can share to your network, but the audio because it's a weekly episode there is a long list of previously recorded episodes in front of you.

Them: What if I don't want to do video just audio.

Me: Then it won't happen. As I do video and audio.

Them: But others offer audio only.

Me: Well then...ask to be on their podcast.

Them: So you don't want me on your podcast?

Me: Let me bottom line it for you: it's my podcast and my rules.

Them: I don't understand what that means.

Me: Ok let me simplify it for you...NO!

Them: I don't understand. I think I would make a great episode for your podcast.

Me: I guess we will never know now.

Them: Will you reconsider?

Me: No.

Them: So you won't reconsider?

Me: What part of NO don't you understand?

Them: Well you don't have to be rude about it.

Me: Apparently I do.

Them: Well I didn't really want to be on your stupid podcast anyway.

Me: Well that's 10 minutes of my life I'm never getting back.

{wait for it....}

Them: F-You!

{and they blocked me}

Note: To make life easier for me I batch record 8-12 episodes at a time. Meaning in most cases there is a 2-3 month delay for when the audio hits podcast channels.

Third Time Is NOT A Charm

Three times this week I have unsubscribed from the same darn email newsletter that I know darn well I never subscribed to begin with and all three times I get this message...

"You have successfully unsubscribed from ALL notifications!"

They might as well say...
"You have successfully unsubscribed from ALL notifications until we send you more tomorrow."

Note: Third time is honestly quite annoying. If you send out emails using a system and that system doesn't remove subscribers when they request so, you the sender can get some very unwelcomed and somewhat angry messages. So, my suggestion is, test your email service and make sure the system actually does indeed remove emails when requested.

Chapter 3

Why Did You Reach Out?

"We Have A Mission For You…
oh, and you're going to have so much fun with it."

Just Say No To Side Hustles

Hey Rob, you should think about a side hustle.

Me: Why?

Them: You'd be good at it.

Me: Why?

Them: You'd make more money.

Me: So you don't think I make enough in the digital media business I currently own?

Them: I'm sure you make plenty, but that's your main hustle, you need a side hustle.

Me: So do you have a side hustle?

Them: I have 3 of them.

Me: So which one gets your primary focus?

Them: All of them.

Me: Doubtful.

Them: Why do you say doubtful?

Me: A side hustle is just that a side hustle - it's something you do when you aren't focusing on your passion project. You can't have 3 side hustles and serve each one equally, one will always be the dominant - and that one is the one that brings you more joy, or money or freedom or whatever.

Them: I have no idea what you're saying.

Me: Exactly, you focused on the wrong thing. Instead of focusing on YOU and building that one thing that supports you financially that brings you joy and freedom...you focused on the idea that hustling is what you need to do.

Them: You don't know what you're talking about.

Me: Don't I...why did you reach out to me?

Them: Well, you have an established business, you're good at marketing and I thought you'd be a good candidate for this opportunity, but you just want to talk passion and freedom.

Me: Okay, first of all why not lead with the opportunity instead of asking me to think about a side hustle. Second, why does everyone pushing a hustle always approach those with established businesses. And finally, I created this business so I would never need a side hustle.

Them: You don't get it. Anyone of my side hustles would have been a great opportunity for you. You could have been great at this.

Me: In 12 months if you are still hustling any of those opportunities show me how much each one has made you and maybe I'll consider it.

Them: These opportunities are now, not in 12 months.

Me: If I charged $100 to listen to everyone's side hustle my mortgage and household expenses would be paid for every month.

Them: You're stupid no wonder you don't have a side hustle.

Me: You didn't listen to anything I said did you?

Them: F-You.

Note: Build your business or someone will hire you to build theirs.

I'm The Team Leader

I'm an A Team captain...not a B Team player.

Them: What does that mean, Rob?

Me: I lead the team, I'm not a bench warmer for your current team.

Them: B Team? Benchwarmer? What?

Me: Look I appreciate the call, but who you want is someone who will follow your lead and do as you say. I'm not an employee and definitely not a YES man.

Them: We haven't even told you what it pays.

Me: Does it pay more than XXXXX a month?

Them: A month, ah no, maybe for 6 months.

Me: See, you don't even value the job enough to hire a C player let alone a B player.

Them: Someone will take it, people are hungry for work.

Me: Well good luck with that.

Them: But we'd really appreciate you helping us.

Me: And I'd really appreciate being treated as the team leader and you paying me what I'm worth.

Them: Can we talk about it?

Me: What have we been doing?

Them: Oh I thought we were negotiating.

Me: I'll make it easy for you...

{I hung up}

Note: Unfortunately, he is right...people are hungry, and when hungry, will accept just about anything. Sad, isn't it? But what's really sad is that there are people who will exploit other's hunger and offer them a pittance knowing full well it's not enough. And these exploiters will continue to do it for as long as they can get away with it.

Have Your Team Do That

Hey Rob, can you help us with SEO?

(Chat I received)

Me: Sure what's your website?

Them: {shares URL}

Me: {glances at website} Hey, I noticed you offer SEO services, so why ask for my help?

Them: We need more clients and we aren't ranking well.

Me: So you want me to optimize your website to get more clients?

Them: Yes.

Me: And you want to pay me to rank your site better so the people searching think you do a great job with your SEO that they will hire you to do theirs?

Them: Yes, of course!

Me: And will you continue to pay me to help you when your clients need SEO services?

Them: No, our team can handle that.

Me: So why isn't your team handling getting your website ranked?

Them: They don't know what you know.

Me: That's true, so why are they helping your clients with their SEO?

Them: Because they pay us too.

Me: Yeah, but if your people really don't know what they are doing how can you ethically provide the service?

Them: Well, they know some things.

Me: Yeah apparently not enough to get you more work.

Them: I don't need a lecture on ethics I need help with SEO, can you help me?

Me: NO!

Them: Why not?

Me: It would be unethical for me to help you deceive people.

Them: I don't care about that.

Me: I do.

Them: I want help with SEO.

Me: Ask your team.

Them: Forget it

Me: Already forgotten.

Them: I don't think you want my work.

Me: Not from people who rip off others, no.

Them: We don't rip them off, they pay what they agreed to pay.

Me: But you aren't delivering the proper service.

Them: What would you charge?

Me: I don't want to help you.

Them: Okay, but if you did help us what would you charge?

Me: I wouldn't help you.

Them: But if you did, what's the price?

Me: {tosses out a number}

Them: We can't afford that?

Me: I know.

Them: F-You.

Me: Have your team do that.

{and I was unfriended and blocked}

Note: In 2014, I partnered with Paul Douglas to coauthor "Optimize This: How Two Carpet Cleaners Consistently Beat Web Designers On The Search Engines." Paul and I took our experience and created a reference book that others could emulate and use to rank their websites. That book is now many years old, however the concepts in the book are still very relevant and still work to rank websites. Oh and yes both Paul and I were former carpet cleaners who sold our businesses to pursue helping others learn digital marketing.

No, Get Out!

Sir you're not wearing a mask.

Me: Yes I know, and might I add you have great observation skills.

Clerk: Why?

Me: Why what?

Clerk: Why aren't you?

Me: What?

Clerk: Why aren't you wearing a mask?

Me: I have a medical condition.

Clerk: What is it?

Me: Are you a doctor?

Clerk: No, but I'm curious.

Me: Well I suffer from sarcasm, so you'd better step back.

Clerk: Get out.

Me: No, really Sarcasm is a huge problem with people like me.

Clerk: Get out.

Me: I'm serious, do you want me to show you my sarcasm card.

Clerk: Your what, no get out.

Note: Sarcasm seems to be a bigger fear than I expected.

We Only Hire Local

Hi Rob, you were referred to me by a mutual friend.

Me: Great. How can I help you?

Them: Well I'm the Manager of (names company) and we need to improve the SEO on our website.

Me: {quick googling the name} Oh, that's an impressive website, but sadly as you realize it has terrible optimization.

Them: Can we meet for coffee?

Me: A video call would be better.

Them: I like to meet all potential vendors for coffee.

Me: Well, that will be difficult as I'm 2,000 miles away in Pennsylvania.

Them: You mean you don't live in my town?

Me: No, not sure why you would assume that.

Them: Well, I just figured since our mutual friend lives near me he would give me the name of someone local.

Me: Apparently, there is no one local that can do what I do, so he gave you my name as the best resource to solve your problem.

Them: We only support local.

Me: I get it, but when you don't have someone local, and you need the service done then you call the person who can do the best job.

Them: We will just wait until a local person is found.

Me: That's up to you, but how long will you wait? I could have your website optimized and making you money or you can continue to wait and lose out on sales.

{ I think you know how it ended. }

Moral of the story: We all want a good deal and we want to support our local economy. However, time waits for no one. And most times it's better to hire the person most qualified so you can be profitable now. Any savings from waiting is diminished with every lost sale.

Invite Declined

Hey Rob I have an invite for you for Clubhouse.
{message received in my FB inbox}

Me: No thanks.

Them: Dude, you're missing out, Clubhouse is the shit.

Me: Then definitely no.

Them: WTF man, I thought you were this big time influencer.

Me: I never considered myself an influencer.

Them: But you have a podcast, you write books, you help clients, you have lots of followers...you have influence.

Me: Having influence and being an influencer is two different things.

Them: Do you want this invite or not?

Me: I already gave you my answer.

Them: You should at least try it before saying no.

Me: You said it's shit...so NO.

Them: WTF shit means it's da bomb.

Me: Again No.

Them: What would convince you to join?

Me: I see you don't understand the concept of No...so for shits and giggles if I did decide to join the invite needs to come from one of these 5 people... The Pope, The President, "Weird Al" Yankovic, my 9th grade biology teacher or Elon Musk

Them: Dude, your an idiot.

Me: It's you're.

Them: What?

Me: If you're going to insult me use proper grammar.

Them: F-You.
{and I was blocked}

Note: The Joy of Missing Out (JOMO) is actually how people should live their lives. Unfortunately it's the Fear of Missing Out (FOMO) that compels them to follow the crowd and do what everyone else is doing. It really is okay not to do what others are doing. It's okay to follow your own path, be your own self and do what you want to do.

No Decision Maker Here

May I speak to the person in charge of making decisions?

Me: He quit last week, we are currently hiring for a new decision maker, however since none of us can make decisions we are not sure how to hire such a person. I can take your name and contact info and when a decision maker is hired, he/she can decide if it's relevant to call you back, okay?

Note: When cold calling a business it's always a good point to know who it is you wish to speak to before placing the call. Asking the person answering the call who the person in charge is just invokes a sarcastic response and you end up in someone's book. Enhance your cold calling skills by learning how to address the right person when you call so you don't end up regretting why you called in the first place.

Chapter 4

Working For Free!

"Trust me, you'll make millions."

Not Registered With Amazon Alexa

Phone rings...caller ID displays SPAM/RISK.

You know me...I have to answer it.

"Don't hang up...your business is not registered with Amazon Alexa - press 1 to be connected to an agent".

Me: {pressing 1}

Not Amazon: Hello Sir, are you familiar with Amazon Alexa?

Me: Well I've heard of her, just never met her in person.

Not Amazon: Sir, it's a voice automated system that listens and adjusts commands to your needs.

Me: Right, didn't Arnold Schwarzenegger star in that movie?

Not Amazon: Sir, it's not a movie, it's a voice system that can be used for all kinds of things. In your case we want to get your business listed when people search your name.

Me: Most people can't pronounce my name, so how will Alexa know what people are asking.

Not Amazon: She will know.

Me: How's it work?

Not Amazon: The system records your business name, address, phone number and zip code and when people are searching using their voice can find you based on those criteria.

Me: Okay but 99% of my business is not local so how will Alexa help me.

Not Amazon: She'll know how to help.

Me: Okay very vague, what's the cost?

Not Amazon: In most cases there is no cost.

Me: What do you mean there is no cost?

Not Amazon: In most cases the set up takes just a few minutes and doesn't require much effort.

Me: So there's no cost?

Not Amazon: That's right, Sir.

Me: So let me get this straight, you call random companies to tell them about Amazon Alexa, then tell them there is no cost, so how do you make money? What's the catch?

Not Amazon: There is no catch.

Me: There is always a catch. No scammer worth his weight is going to work for free.

{they hung up...was it something I said}

Note: Any call that starts off with "don't hang up"…just hang up. It's most likely a scam. And when they mention Amazon Alexa and there's no catch, then it's definitely a scam. Don't fall for it.

Virtual Nonsense

Hey Rob you should sign up for my virtual event.

{message I received in my FB chat}

Me: I see you virtually every day.

Them: Yes, but this an event.

Me: So basically more of you just virtually.

Them: Well, I'll be teaching cool stuff.

Me: You post stuff every day, again virtually.

Them: You're missing the point.

Me: Am I? It's you teaching...virtually. You post stuff every day. Why the need for an event?

Them: I think it's needed.

Me: What I think is needed is we drop the virtual crap and have real life events again, where real people meet and prospect.

Them: That seems so unsafe.

Me: What's unsafe is living in a virtual world thinking you can grow your business.

Them: You just don't understand.

Me: Okay smarty pants tell me how many people signed up for your virtual event and how much are you charging for it?

Them: It's a free event and I have 20 people signed up.

Me: Free you say? Wow, I bet that'll pay a lot of bills.

Them: Again you don't understand.

Me: Oh, I know the power of FREE, but every day you are giving FREE with your posts and now you want to do a FREE event that will make you nothing.

Them: My plan is to sell them on my coaching program.

Me: You can't even convince me to join your FREE event. How are you going to convince people to shell out their hard earned money for your coaching program?

{wait for it....}

Them: F-You

{and I was unfriended and blocked}

Note: People love FREE stuff…it's a fact. But are the ones attracted to FREE stuff actually fit to be your client? Most of the time that answer is NO. Eventually you have to learn that FREE doesn't pay your bills and you need to charge for your time.

Zoom, Zoom

Hi Rob! I'm doing research on Business trends and discovered that getting in front of new potential clients is a major challenge in the market. Is that the case for you also? I'm finding a lot of useful content and industry insights in my research lately. Would you be interested in chatting about them over a Zoom call next week? ~James
{message I received through LinkedIn 5 minutes after accepting this person as a connection}

Me: I charge $500 per 1/2 hour for Zoom calls. I have a few openings next week, when is good for you?

James: It will take more than 1/2 hour to share with you the research. And I certainly don't wish to pay $500.

Me: Well more time equals more charge so if you need an hour the fee will be $1000.

James: No, I will not be paying you to Zoom.

Me: Well technically you will be paying PayPal and PayPal will forward the money to me.

James: I don't think you understand what I'm offering.

Me: If it's not payment for my time, then I'm not interested.

James: You're incredulous.

Me: And that concludes our research today.

{and I got unfriended and blocked}

Note: If you're using LinkedIn to network, learn how to connect without being creepy or annoying.

Chapter 5

Wasn't Me

"And you can't prove it."

Why Did You Delete My Comment

Hey Rob why did you delete my comment from your post?

{was the message that popped up on my FB messenger}

Me: What comment?

Them: Didn't you see it?

Me: Again, what comment?

Them: Oh, you didn't see what I posted?

Me: I get notifications when people comment, share or like. I never saw one that said you did anything on any comment I posted.

Them: Your Facebook must be broken.

Me: How much have you've been smoking?

Them: I haven't smoked anything today.

Me: Did you forget to take your meds today? Or perhaps you took too much.

Them: What are you saying?

Me: How can I delete something I know nothing about?

Them: Dude, you did something. My post isn't there.

Me: {scanning his friends list} Maybe it was another Rob whose post you commented on.

Them: It was yours I know it.
{shares the subject and what his comment was}

Me: Wasn't me. I never posted anything like that.

Them: You did. And now the entire post is gone.

Me: I think you need to have your meds checked.

Them: Dude, stop saying that, I'm not paranoid.

Me: Just delusional.

Them: F-you A-hole.

{20 minutes later}

Them: Hey, it wasn't you, it was another Rob.

Me: See I told you.

Them: Jerk!

Me: Make sure you adjust your meds.

Them: Stop being an A-Hole.

Me: Stop doing drugs.

{and I got unfriended and blocked}

Public Service Announcement: Mixing drugs with social media doesn't work…ever. Just don't do it. Seriously, whomever told you it's a good idea is wrong. Stop listening to those people. Just lay off the drugs.

Just Admit It

Hi Sir this is Card Services

Me: Again?

Card Services: Sir?

Me: You just called me a few minutes ago.

Card Services: Sir? No Sir!

Me: Yup, you did.

Card Services: Sir, I assure you this is the first time I'm calling you.

Me: How much you willing to bet?

Card Services: Sir?

Me: Stop Sir'ing me and just admit you called me earlier.

Card Services: Sir, I have no idea what you are talking about.

Me: Same accent, same lame play dumb tactics - it was you.

Card Services: Sir?

Me: I said stop Sir'ing me. Just admit it was you.

Card Services: Sir I'll call you again tomorrow okay.

{He hung up}

Note: Any time someone calls you saying they are with "Card Services" just hang up…it's a scam.

Chapter 6

Easily Offended

"Prepare to be triggered."

Apparently My Tone Was Awful

YEEEEESSSSS!

So love starting the day having both offended and triggered someone because of my "tone".

This person suggested in a Facebook group that raw unedited video files produced by a contractor should be handed over to the client when the contract is ended. This person suggested "they will look good for it".

Well you know me...I had to give my two cents.

Me: How does looking good pay her bills? I hate that term "you'll look good for it" as if some karma angel is watching your back and keeping score of all your good. Pfft.

Them: (writes 2 long winded comments as to her 8 years of experience, how much she charges and that "the client might come back or refer them in the future")

Me: So you run your company your way, and I'll run my company my way. But don't get all indignant when people disagree with your thinking. That's life. Not everyone believes in mystic karma and that doing "good" pays off.

Them: Oh gosh Rob. That's kind of aggressive. You made an assumption about my approach so I wanted to explain where I was coming from. You do you. But aggression and name calling is highly unprofessional. We're always entitled to disagree, of course, but aggression is an ugly trait. It seems you are aggressive at my disagreeing with you. No problem, take care of yourself and good karma to you.

Me: Aggression? Name calling? I neither exhibited aggression nor called you a name.

Them: I'm going to end this here Rob, your tone was awful. I wish you well.

Me: My tone was awful? Wow you certainly get offended easily.

Them: I'm the least offended person ever, lol! I just didn't like your tone! It was a bit shitty really! As I said, I wish you well!

Me: And you needed to further comment? You said you were ending it. Ending means not continuing.

{and I was reported to Facebook, and the person then unfriended and blocked me}

Note: Facebook does certainly bring out the best in people. Yup, they were the best at being offended, easily triggered, indignant and passive aggressive.

You Are A Business Of Some Sort Right

HomeAdvisor just called me.

They called on a spoofed local number.

Me: Hello

HA: Hi we wanted to see if we can help you?

Me: With what?

HA: Get more business.

Me: Do you know what we do?

HA: Well, we know you are a business of some sort that probably needs more customers, right?

Me: I don't need you.

HA: All businesses could use some help.

Me: Not from you.

HA: Sir, you don't know how we work.

Me: And you have no clue what we do.

HA: Sir, if you can share with me more about you I'm sure we can help.

Me: Next time know what we do before calling me.

HA: So you won't let me help you.

Me: I've already said I don't need your service.

HA: Well you don't have to be so rude.

Me: RUDE is calling someone and not knowing what they do and continuing to yammer on.

HA: I don't think we can help you.

Me: That's a real shame.
{they hung up}

Note: When a company calls you on a spoofed number that is a clear indication that they are not being authentic. Add in the fact that when they call they have no clue on who you are or what your business does, it's time to just hang up…or stay on the line and waste their time. I think you know my choice.

Your Coach Is An Idiot

Hey Rob...
{was the message I received from a new connection in my Facebook messenger}

Me: No

Them: Well you don't even know what I'm going to say.

Me: We've been connections for what... maybe 5 minutes... and you're probably going to send me some link to check out or tell me to buy your newest course or how great your coaching is, right?

Them: Well I did want to tell you about our seminar coming up.

Me: Yup, and that seminar has a link right?

Them: Of course, you will need to sign up.

Me: Oh I won't need to sign up, I don't even want you to share it with me.

Them: Did I get you on a bad day, I can check back next week.

Me: My answer next week will be the same.

Them: Oh so you're not interested.

Me: Let me ask you - does connecting with someone and immediately sending them a message inviting them to your seminar work?

Them: I spend 2-3 hours a day connecting with people and letting them know about my seminar. It's a numbers game, some will say yes and some won't.

Me: And how many actually say yes?

Them: Honestly, not many.

Me: Then why do it?

Them: My coach says I need to.

Me: Your coach is an idiot.

Them: I pay a lot of money to my coach.

Me: And that makes you... an idiot too.

Them: Dude, you're rude.

Me: Really, rude is connecting with people and then spamming them without ever trying to learn how you can actually help them.

Them: F-You

{and I was unfriended and blocked}

Note: I know a lot of brilliant coaches and none of them will ever say you need to spam people with garbage pitches. One of the things I do when I connect with someone on social media is I send them a message along with a 15 second video.

Hey hey...
I recorded a quick 15 second video
...don't worry I'm not pitching anything.
(I so dislike those people too)
Just wanted to introduce myself and wish you well.
 http://bit.ly/RobsConnectionVideo

Here's the transcript to that video...
"Hey this Rob Anspach, I just wanted to say thanks for the connection. I appreciate you and look forward to having an awesome conversation with you. Have a great day."

I Failed His Personality Test

Hey Rob, did you ever take one of those personality tests?

{message I received in my FB chat}

Me: Yup

Them: What was the verdict?

Me: I have one!

Them: One what?

Me: A personality.

Them: Lol no, what four letter classification did you score?

Me: Oh that personality test. Yeah took it long ago.

Them: Awesome, what was the verdict?

Me: Why?

Them: I'm curious.

Me: Well I'm curious as to why?

Them: I think it's important in my decision making.

Me: Your decision making regarding what?

Them: Hiring you.

Me: And you started out with "did you ever take a personality test" to determine if I'm worthy of being hired?

Them: Yes, I ask every vendor that question before hiring them.

Me: And does it work?

Them: Most of the time.

Me: Not interested.

Them: I haven't told you what I need or what I'm willing to pay.

Me: First, I don't care. And second, I still don't care. And third, we are not a good fit.

Them: So apparently your personality is one to avoid then?

Me: For you yes.

Them: How do people even deal with you?

Me: Why are you still chatting?

Them: I'm trying to figure you out.

Me: So you're analyzing me, good luck with that.

Them: I've never come across someone so rude.

Me: Seems that today's your lucky day.

Them: F-You

Me: Hah, was waiting for that!

Them: You're a jerk.

Me: And that's why you fail as an entrepreneur, you have a sensitive personality not suited to dealing with jerks like me.

Them: F-You

{and I was blocked}

Note: I've been an entrepreneur for over 25 years and I have never used a personality test to qualify an employee, a vendor or even a client. Maybe it works for some people. But I have to believe that if someone asked you, before you even established what they needed, what your personality index was you'd probably tell them to kick rocks.

I Am Mean

Hi Rob, I was doing some research and came across your profile.

I have a few ideas I want to share that can help you grow your coaching business! Would love to connect & chat with you!

{message I received on LinkedIn}

Me: Doing research you say? Came across my profile did ya? You have a few ideas that you want to share with me, okay, first question...do you even know who I am?

Them: Yes, you're an authority builder.

Me: And that means what to you?

Them: You help people.

Me: Help them do what?

Them: These questions seem ridiculous.

Me: Getting spammed with dumb messages saying how you can help me when you don't even know who I am or what I do is ridiculous.

Them: Well maybe I don't want you to be a connection anymore.

Me: Maybe? Are you not sure? I know I'd prefer if you weren't a connection.

Them: You seem mean.

Me: I am mean, now go away.

{and I got blocked}

Note: Don't you just love when someone sends you an unsolicited message saying how they can help you when they evidently have no clue what you do? And it seems these LinkedIn spammers all subscribe to the same guru who tells them what template to use. It's crazy. Yet, they continue to do it. So, being the nice guy I am, I've taken it upon myself (sort of my mission) to straighten out these LinkedIn losers and let them know that their behavior is no longer tolerated. Do they listen? Not really. But it does provide brilliant material for these books…so there's that.

Chapter 7

Trying To Scam Me?

"Do or do not, there is no try." ~Yoda

Pfft, Not Leo's Brother

Hi this is Sasha from Visa/Mastercard calling to offer you a 0% interest rate - press 1 to secure your low interest rate today.

(says the recorded message)

Me: {pressing 1}

Scammer: What is the expiration date of your credit card?

Me: Sure, but first who are you?

Scammer: We are Visa Mastercard services representing Chase, Bank of America and 297 other banking entities worldwide.

Me: I asked who you are, not what you did?

Scammer: I'm Mark

Me: Mark what? What's your last name?

Scammer: DiCaprio.

Me: DiCaprio? So you're Leo's brother?

Scammer: Leo who?

Me: I can't believe you've forgotten who your brother is.

Scammer: My brother is Faruq.

Me: Never heard of him.

Scammer: Who is Leo?

Me: Leo? Most people call him Leonardo DiCaprio.

Scammer: Sir, what is the credit card you want to get a lower rate on.

Me: Dude, forget about my credit card, you need my help. I need to reacquaint you with your long lost brother Leo.

Scammer: To hell with Leo.

Me: That's not a very nice thing to say about your brother.

Scammer: My brother is Faruq, not Leo.

Me: Faruq is a bad influence on you, you're much better off getting to know your other brother Leo.

Scammer: {curses at me in some Pakistani dialect}

Me: So you're not with Visa Mastercard and I bet dollars to donuts DiCaprio isn't even your last name. Are you trying to scam me?

Scammer: F-You Mother F-er

{scammer hangs up}

Note: The whole Rob Versus series started with "Rob Versus The Scammers" – and I still have fun messing with scammers. Especially ones who get flustered so fast.

This Is The IRS

Local number appeared on my Caller ID
{I knew it was a scam...but you know me, I just had to answer it}

Me: Hello

(automatic message)
Hi this is the IRS, please press 1 to speak to an agent.
{so I did}

{Dude with a thick foreign accent answers}
Hello may I help you?

Me: You called me.

Sir, can I get your first name and last name?

Me: So in the time you dialed my number to the time I pressed 1 to be switched to you, you've forgotten my name?

Sir, are you wasting my time?

Me: You called me.

Sir this is the IRS.

Me: In this case the IRS stands for Idiots Remembering Squat.

F-You Mother F-er
{he hung up}

Note: The real IRS (Internal Revenue Service) will never call you from a local number, and probably never at all. Usually all communication is via letters mailed through the USPS.

Grab A Pen And Paper

I was outside walking the dog when my cell phone rings.

I glanced at the caller ID and knew it was a scam call, but I just had to answer.

It was the travel award scammers offering me a fantastic Mexico vacation.

Me: Hello

Scammer Dude: Hi Sir, I see you stayed on the line to get more information, how are you today?

Me: Well I'm outside walking the dog.

Scammer Dude: Well that's great, now can you grab a pen and paper as I have some special destinations and details I want to share with you.

Me: A pen and paper you say?

Scammer Dude: Yes Sir, I can wait while you grab those.

Me: I'm outside walking the dog. Where do you suppose I'm going to find a pen and some paper?

Scammer Dude: I can wait.

Me: Are you not understanding me? I'm outside. No pen. No paper. Just me walking the dog.

Scammer Dude: That's okay, I can wait.

Me: Wait for what? Are you beaming some paper and pen over to my exact location?

Scammer Dude: Sir, you seem frustrated, are you not able to find a pen and paper.

Me: Nope, sorry there is no pen and paper available.

Scammer Dude: Well that's okay... I'd be glad to share the details of the package with you.

Me: Without the pen and paper, I'm thinking you might get in trouble.

Scammer Dude: Are you making fun of me?

Me: Oh, now you're listening.

Scammer Dude: I heard you, but I must follow the script.

Me: Well you can stick the script along with a pen and some paper up your...

{he hung up}

Note: During the pandemic when travel was being restricted I received so many calls saying I won or was being awarded some trip. A trip that would have required congressional hearings to drop restrictions for anyone to even travel. Hey, getting a great deal on a vacation is something most people will find appealing. Unfortunately, accepting a travel award from a total stranger will most likely end with you getting scammed.

Agent M The Health Insurance Scammer

Discovery Health Network just called me...

Me: Hello.

DHN: Hi, I'm Tina from Discovery Health Network and we wanted to let you know we have a team ready to help you with your health insurance needs.

Me: Okay.

DHN: We are currently enrolling and need to ask you a few questions, is that okay?

Me: Sure.

DHN: Are you currently enrolled in Medicare, Medicaid or Social Security Disability?

Me: Nope.

DHN: Great I think you qualify?

Me: You asked me one question.

DHN: Sir, we asked you several questions?

Me: You asked me about Medicare, Medicaid and Disability.

DHN: Sir, that was three separate questions.

Me: That was one question with three options.

DHN: Sir, you seem combative this morning.

Me: I'm always combative.

DHN: I will transfer to another agent

Me: 007 perhaps?

DHN: This is Malinda, how may I help you?

Me: Can I call you M?

DHN: Sir what are you talking about?

Me: You're Agent M!

DHN: Sir, I believe you're confused.

Me: So the first call taker says I'm combative and you say I'm confused, which is it?

DHN: Sir, do you need health insurance, or are you wasting our time?

Me: You called me, so are you going to try to sell me health insurance or continue insulting me?

{grr, the bastards hung up}

Note: Again, a random caller who knows nothing of you except what you share when they are trying to sell you on something you probably don't need. And if you give them your pertinent information (such as credit card, banking accounts or social security number) they will most likely use it in nefarious ways.

Scammer Might Have Covid

This is a call from your electric utility company, we see you have been over paying for your consumption, to get a $50 refund and a 35% bill reduction press 1 now.

{You know me...}

Me: {Pressing 1}

Scammer: {COUGH, COUGH} Hi, This is {COUGH, COUGH} Sam.

Me: Who?

Scammer: {Clears throat, coughs again} This is Sam. How are you?

Me: I'm fine, but you sound sick.

Scammer: {cough, cough, cough} I'm fine, just a cough.

Me: Well, Sam you are coughing in my ear.

Scammer: Sorry, I will try not to {cough, cough} cough in your ear.

Me: Well, how about you call me back when you don't have Covid.

Scammer: I don't have Covid.

{I thought for sure the call would end there, but nope... Sam's buddy gets on the line.}

Scammer 2: This is Steve, I can help you with your electric rate.

Me: Where's Sam?

Scammer 2: I have relieved Sam, I will be helping you now.

Me: Sam sounds really sick. I hope he gets better.

Scammer 2: Forget about Sam, let me help you.

Me: Do you think Sam has Covid? If Sam has Covid, then you might have Covid too.

Scammer 2: {Steve raises his voice} SAM DOESN'T HAVE COVID, I DON'T HAVE COVID.

{the whole call center goes quiet}

Me: Sounds like you are upset, maybe you need anger management.

Scammer 2: F-YOU

Me: So, I take it, no electric rate reduction then?

Scammer 2: {mumbles several foreign curse words, I won't repeat}

Me: So not only do you have Covid, and anger issues you need to get your mouth washed out with soap too.

Scammer 2: F-You Mother F-er.

{he hangs up on me}

Note: Anytime the call starts off with "this is a call from your electric utility company" without actually mentioning the name of said company…it's a scam. Don't reveal any information. Just hang up. Or channel what you learned in this book and just completely waste their time.

State Of Confusion

Hi this is Eve with Discovery Health Network.

Are you currently on Medicare, Medicaid or Social Security Disability?

Me: Nope

Eve: Great let me transfer you to a representative.

Rep: Hi what State are you currently in.

Me: Confusion.

Rep: Say again.

Me: Confusion.

Rep: Sir, that is not a valid answer.

Me: You asked what state I was currently in...not what State I reside in.

Rep: Do you want insurance or not?

Me: Are they the only 2 options?

Rep: What options? What are you talking about?

Me: You asked if I want insurance that is option 1 and or not is option 2.

Rep: You're stupid.

Me: As I tried to tell you...State of Confusion

Rep: I believe you are wasting my time.

Me: What gave it away?
{pfft, they hung up}

Note: Scamming people on Medicare, Medicaid and Social Security Disability is a big business. And sadly, scammers know how to sound convincing. Don't be a victim. Learn to protect yourself and your loved ones against these scams.

I'm Not The Customer You Are Looking For

Hi is this Mr. Stafford

{the caller asked - how my mobile number got associated with Mr. Stafford I'll never know - but you know me...I played along}

Me: Why yes, how may I help you?

Caller: This is Jim from American Solar.
{he said with a thick foreign accent}

Me: American Solar you say, where are you located?

Caller: We are located in the United States.

Me: Wow, that's nice.

Caller: How much do you pay for electricity in Camp Hill?
{must be where Mr. Stafford lives}

Me: Oh, around $200 a month give or take

Caller: Give or take, what does that mean?

Me: What, you never heard that term before...it means sometimes I give more and sometimes they take more. Get it, got it, good.

Caller: Not really, but let's continue. Your first name is Annie right?
{so apparently he knows I'm a Mister as he addressed me that way, but whatever...I'll go with it.}

Me: Yes, that's right Annie, which is short for Anakin.

Caller: That's a strange name.

Me: Yup, it was given to me by my father George Lucas Stafford.

Caller: That name sounds familiar.

Me: You probably called him, I'm sure you make lots of calls. And they force you to adhere to a script, and you can't go dark side and adlib like you are doing now. You might get taken before the council and banished.

Caller: Sir, Anakin Sir...err, hmm, Mr. Stafford, I have no idea what you are saying.

Me: Ah, well the force is weak with you then.

Caller: I don't understand.

Me: I'm not the customer you are looking for.

Caller: You're not the customer I'm looking for, what? Sir, do you want our solar package or not? I'm not understanding what you are talking about.

Me: Apparently you are still a Padawan, a learner, a student...and haven't mastered the art of scam calling people yet.

Caller: F You Anakin

Me: Noooooooooooo!

{pfft he hung up - I so wish these foreign scammers would understand Star Wars references}

Note: If you can confuse them, get them off script and use the force on them…it makes for a fun conversation.

I Guess Fhloston Paradise Isn't An Option

So the travel awards scammers called telling me all the places I could use their service so I asked...

Me: Does it include a week at Club Med on Fhloston Paradise?

Caller: Yup, wherever I wanted to go.

Me: Am I getting a Multi-Pass?

Caller: Yup, yup.

Me: Will my host at the resort be Ruby Rhod?

Caller: Hmm, wait a minute this sounds familiar... did you just Fifth Element me?

Me: Big Ba-da Boom

They hung up.

Note: The Fifth Element is a science fiction movie starring Bruce Willis that came out in 1997, which I may have watched close to 100 times. So yeah, I kind of know all the lines. But I knew all that time spent watching that movie would come in handy one day. And it did. Hundreds of hours of watch time to be used on a 5 minute call. Oh, it was so worth it.

It's A Fake Page

I see someone post one of those fake page giveaways - so I tell them it's a fake page.

(You know the ones... RV giveaways, car giveaways, house giveaways.)

Them: Can you show me proof, I can't find anything.

Me: Here's proof... {shows them real page versus fake page comparisons}

Them: Well the page you say is fake has 48,000 followers so it must be okay.

Me: It's a fake page designed to look like the real page in order to gather your name and information.

{unfriends me}

Then Facebook displays a pop up that says, "*The Post Has Been Removed: the post or object that you were commenting has been removed by its owner and can no longer be commented on.*"

Note: I don't want people to be scammed, I even wrote a book dedicated to helping people fight scams - so when I tell you it's a scam, believe me. I'm trying to protect you.

Chapter 8

PITA's Everywhere

"And it's not the good kind of Pita!"

We Really Want You & Your Team To Help Us

Hey Rob, I really want you to help me.

Me: Okay, so what's the problem?

Them: Well you quoted me X,XXX

Me: And?

Them: My budget is set at XXX

Me: Well you have two choices (1) increase your budget or (2) find someone cheaper

Them: Well I really want you and your team to help us.

Me: Great I'll send an invoice for my service.

Them: No, our budget isn't set for that.

Me: Then find someone cheaper.

Them: So you won't work with us for a lesser amount?

Me: I gave you two choices.

Them: Yeah, but we want to hire you.

Me: Okay, I'll make it simple…call someone else.

Them: So, you're turning away a paying client.

Me: No I'm turning away a PITA (pain in the ass) who doesn't value what I do and just wants a cheaper price.

Them: You're a dumbass.

Me: Really? And to think you wanted to hire this dumbass to help you with your marketing.

Them: F-You.

Note: I stopped asking a long time ago what someone's budget is because (1) they might not know, (2) they have it set way too low or (3) they are basing it on false or misleading information. And frankly, when you ask someone what their arbitrary budget is you try to formulate a price that meets their requirement. Well that's a quick way to go bankrupt. So I don't even ask. I tell them this is my price and if they can afford it, great, we do business. If they can't afford it, no problem, they can go somewhere else. Never ever let the potential client dictate what they will pay you.

I Don't Need It, But They Want Me To Have It

Home phone rings...it's PayPal.

Me: Hello

PayPal: Hi Sir is this Robert?

Me: Yeah, but why are calling on my home line?

PayPal: That number is associated with your account.

Me: My business line and my cell phone are associated with the account, my home line is only associated with my name for security purposes not for soliciting.

PayPal: That's not what we have on file.

{me logging into my PayPal account}

Me: I'm looking at my account and what I told you is true.

PayPal: Okay, whatever you say.

Me: Why are you calling me?

PayPal: We want to offer you a business line of credit up to $29k

Me: I don't need it.

PayPal: But Covid has ruined businesses all over and most need the capital.

Me: My business wasn't ruined and I don't need the loan.

PayPal: You sure?

Me: Oh yeah, positive. Didn't asked for it, don't want it.

{I hung up}

{3 minutes later I receive an email from PayPal}

It was great speaking with you today about the PayPal Working Capital business loan. Like we talked about, PayPal Working Capital is a fast and affordable solution for businesses who need cash quickly. To get started go to our website and press Apply Now.

Grr...these people are relentless.

Note: When did NO stop meaning NO and start being considered MAYBE? That's the problem today is that people are taught NO is just a suggestion and to keep asking, or sending messages until they get a YES. Well when I say NO...I mean NO. And, if you persist don't get all indignant when you wind up in one of my books.

No More Apps

Sir in order to get our best deals you should download our app.

Me: I have too many apps, don't want any more.

Store clerk: Well that's your problem then.

Me: Yup, suppose so.

Store clerk: Do you truly need all those apps?

Me: Well they all serve a purpose.

Store clerk: Well if they aren't saving you money at our store then they aren't serving the right purpose.

Me: I'm thinking I don't need your app.

Store clerk: But then you won't get our great deals.

Me: I'll pass

Store clerk: Sir I'm sure there is one app you can delete so you can add ours.

Me: Probably not.

Store clerk: Okay then have at it - delete anyone then download our app.

Me: You know what, I don't want your app...

Store clerk: You need our app.

Me: I need to leave.

Store clerk: Give me your phone and I'll download the app and set it up for you.

Me: I'm going to throat punch you.

{Store clerk yells for security}

{Security now wants to know why I threatened the store clerk with violence. Wonders why I just didn't download the app.}

Note: I love the apps I use. But I'm not going to download an app for a store I will probably never go back to. In the book I coauthored with Lori Ratzlaff called, "No Experience Necessary: Social Media For The Boomers, Gen X-ers & The Over 50 Entrepreneur" we even included a chapter called "It's All About Those Apps".

Bottom line: Apps take up space and memory on your phone and if you don't need the app or haven't used them in several months get rid of them.

Hey A-Hole

Hey A-Hole Why Did You Delete My Comment on Your Post?

{was the message in my FB chat from a non-friend}

Me: I deleted it because I don't know you.

Them: Well you shouldn't have the post set to everyone then.

Me: Well, how about next time you just ignore a post from someone you don't know.

Them: When it's false I will comment.

Me: How was my comment false? It was my about me and what I did in a particular situation.

Them: It wasn't the whole story.

Me: Really? So you were there?

Them: No, and I wasn't even born then. But what you stated wasn't accurate.

Me: And you just wanted to be "that" person to call me out?

Them: Someone had too, and it seemed everyone was cheering for you and I needed to set the record straight.

Me: The record as you see it right?

Them: No, the truth.

Me: Which is?

Them: That you're wrong.

Me: Oh yes, being corrected by someone more than 1/2 my age who isn't even on my friends list, who has never commented on anything I posted before, but now wants to scold me on something I posted which they believe isn't accurate.

Them: You really are an A-hole.

Me: And you seem to be an entitled brat who wasn't spanked enough as a child.

Them: I'm reporting you to Facebook.

Me: Go ahead.

Them: I mean it...I'm reporting you.

Me: And I said go ahead, do it.

Them: Well I'm going to have all my friends monitor your comments and we'll comment and make your life hell.

Me: Awesome...I need more content for my next book.

Them: What? What books?

Me: I write about dumbasses like you and your friends and have a whole series of books that help entrepreneurs learn to avoid your crap.

Them: Oh.

Me: And thank you.

Them: Never mind, sorry to have bothered you. I'll leave you alone now.

Me: Aren't you going to report me?

Them: No.

Me: Why not?

Them: Can you stop replying?

Me: Well you contacted me, now you want me to stop replying?

Them: Look I don't want to continue this. I won't comment on your posts again.

Me: Well you opened Pandora's box...you just can't close it and think nothing happened.

Them: I don't even know what that is. All I did was comment on your post and now you won't leave me alone.

Me: Not only did you comment on my post, but after I deleted it you had the audacity to send me a message calling me an A-Hole.

Them: Stop messaging me.

Me: I can do this all day.

Them: It's harassment.

Me: Is it though?

Them: Now I'm reporting you.

Me: Oh, you didn't report me earlier?

Them: STOP

Me: What am I a text service? I don't do commands.

Them: STOP. STOP. STOP.

Me: You didn't say the magic word.

Them: A-Hole

Me: That's not even close.
{It was then that I got blocked}

As my friend Michelle Woolard Pippin said when this all went down...

"Is it me... or does it FEEL a bit entitled, a bit outrageous, a bit narcissistic... for someone to hop on YOUR Facebook post & argue with your friends?"

Oh My Gawd

Select the perfect item.

Order it. Get email a day later saying perfect item is out of stock.

But, if we accept the same item but with a different color they will deduct $10. We reject their ridiculous offer.

Receive another email saying will deduct $20 if we accept. Reject again. Receive third email saying they will deduct $30.

Now the item in question was priced at $80 and the color choice they wanted us to accept didn't match anything. But apparently they were desperate to get rid of it.

We rejected it again. Get another email saying we can't cancel via email and all cancellations need to be done through website.

Fine. Go to website to cancel order. Then some chatbot comes on asking why we are canceling. Seems not accepting their offer is not an option. After filling out their form with the proper information, I receive a response - "website emails are not monitored in real time, please allow 4-6 weeks for response."

What the bloody hell? Screw it, called my credit card and told them what was happening, they issued a chargeback against vendor.

Not more than 15 minutes later, receive email from vendor saying I messed up their process by calling credit card company direct and they will be adding cancellation fees to my order.

Oh hell no. Called the credit card company back again and this time also sent them copies of all communication with vendor.

Credit card company informed me the vendor tried to charge my card 3 more times.

Chapter 9

One Of Those People

"Well, I made the list...so I have that going for me."

I'm A Big Fat Jerk

Hey Rob, why did unfriend me just now?

{was the message in my Facebook inbox, roughly 10 seconds after I unfriended the person}

Me: Because you are one of those people

Them: One of what people?

Me: Who monitors their friend list and the moment someone decides to unfriend you, you jump all over them with a bunch of questions.

Them: How would you even know that, you just unfriended me.

Me: Oh at the time I didn't, but I do now.

Them: So is this a test or something

Me: If it was, you just failed.

Them: I don't get this whole conversation, you unfriended me, and I'm the one failing.

Me: Yes I unfriended you, leave it at that, now go away.

Them: Was it something I did?

Me: Yes

Them: What?

Me: Why does it matter?

Them: I would like to know.

Me: Well, too bad, not going to tell you. Go Away.

Them: I'm not going away until you tell me why you unfriended me.

Me: How about I just block you, would that be better?

Them: I just don't understand why you are doing this.

Me: If you weren't notified that I unfriended you, would you even care?

Them: That's not the point.

Me: Yes, that is the point. Those programs that tell you the second someone is no longer a friend do nothing to strengthen your own inner emotional wellbeing. In fact, it's better you don't know when someone unfriended you.

Them: Well I always want to know why someone unfriended me so I can improve myself and be better for my new friends.

Me: Bingo...that's why I dissed you. You are not you, you don't even know who you are, you are constantly changing so that you are accepted by all and most of your social media friends probably have no clue what your true personality is.

{And I got blocked - 2 minutes later was sent a message on my LinkedIn from the person telling me I'm a big fat jerk and they were blocking me on all social media now.}

Note: I get it, you want to know why someone unfriended you. But ask yourself, were they really a friend to begin with, or just a social media connection. And if they were just a connection why waste the drama trying to win them back?

One Less Friend

Hey Rob, I would love for you to be one of our trusted affiliates.

{message received through Facebook chat}

Me: Hmm, I haven't heard from you in years.

Them: Oh sorry, I was working for a company for a couple of years but now I'm back on my own.

Me: And you have this wonderful affiliate program you want to tell me all about right?

Them: Oh, yes, we just launched it. It really is amazing.

Me: Great, send me it to try and I'll consider it.

Them: No, you have to buy it first then we sign you up as an affiliate.

Me: So you want me to buy it first?

Them: Yes.

Me: And how much is it?

Them: $49

Me: And how much is the affiliate payout?

Them: 10%

Me: Pass

Them: Why pass?

Me: Why the hell would I be an affiliate if (1) I have to buy it to be an affiliate and (2) the payout is only 10%? It just doesn't make sense.

Them: We are keeping the prices low to attract more people.

Me: That's stupid.

Them: What is?

Me: This whole conversation. Why the heck would anyone want to sell your product if they are only making $4.90?

Them: It's an easy sell. You could easily sell 10 units per week.

Me: If only I could throat punch you.

Them: Why are you so hostile. This is a great deal.

Me: Where's Dr Kevorkian when you need him?

Them: Are saying you want me dead?

Me: Now you are catching on.

Them: I don't know why I even bothered to ask you.

Me: Because the universe said you needed a reality check so ask Rob.

Them: It's a wonder you have friends.

Me: I know right, but today I get to have one less. Goodbye.
{I unfriended and blocked him}

Note: The cheaper the price, the more hassles involved. This one was a train wreck of hassles I was glad to avoid.

Open House Extortion

Real Estate Agent Client calls on a Sunday at 1:23 pm

Client: Shelley, I start an open house at 2 PM. Can you please get it out on all of my social media for me here's the address.

Shelly: I'm sorry we just got out of church and I am with family having dinner. I am not at my office. I'm happy to schedule open houses, but I normally don't work on Sunday and I'm not near a computer.

Client: Fine. I will cancel my service if you don't do it.

Submitted by Shelley Costello, CEO of Creative Web Concepts

Remember: It's your business and your hours... always remember the old saying – *"Poor planning on your part does not necessitate an emergency on mine"*- Bob Carter. Be respectful.

- - - - -

Not My Dentist

Right now I'm getting hit with emails from marketers thinking that I run a dental office. They point to how they will carefully redesign my website to help me get more dental clients. I don't know how to break the news to them that I'm not a dentist.
~ David Holub, Personal Injury Attorney, Indiana
www.davidholublaw.com

Some sage advice (from Faith Sage): Always check out your potential clients before sending them emails, messages or calling them... you might just be surprised about what they do.

If you'd like to be featured in a future Rob Versus book submit your story to RVB@anspachmedia.com

Chapter 10

I'm Sorry, Not!

"I regret your apology and thank you by wasting your time."

Apology Call Meets HWP

An apology call from my supposed electric utility offering me a rebate and 30% discount.

They asked me who my utility company is...

Me: You are calling to offer me an apology for overcharging my account and yet you don't remember what your company name is?

Caller: Sir, we are trying to get you your rebate and we work with hundreds of utilities.

Me: You haven't even told me your name yet?

Caller: My name is Karen.

Me: You don't say.

Caller: Sir, is your electric utility Met Ed, PECO or PPL?

Me: None of those.

Caller: Sir, what is the name of your electric company?

Me: HWP

Caller: Sir can you repeat that.

Me: HWP

Caller: Is that new, what does it stand for?

Me: Hamster Wheel Powered

Caller: Do you know the address of the company and what rate they are charging?

Me: Well...

Caller: Did you say "Hamster"?

Me: Yes Hamster...as in the 4 legged furry rat looking things

Caller: Sir you need to take this seriously.

Me: Oh, yes, scamming people is a serious business.

Caller: F-You!
{scammer hung up}

Ha-ha, HWP gets them every time.

Note: Never, ever give the caller your true electric providers name or any account information as it will be used against you and most likely for nefarious purposes.

Some more sage advice (from Faith Sage): Asking questions really gets to the bottom of things *and fast!* Whether it's for a legitimate business or to uncover a scammer... ask questions.

Another Apology Call

This is an apology call from your utility company, we are calling to inform you overpaid for your consumption.

Please press 1 to get a $50 rebate check and 35% reduction in future bills.

Me: {pressing 1}

Scammer: Hi are you the person in charge of paying the electric and gas bill.

Me: I don't have a gas bill, only an electric bill.

Scammer: What is your zip code.

Me: {telling them the 5 digit zip from a town 25 miles away)

Scammer: Can you repeat that number?

Me: {repeating the number}

Scammer: {rattles off 4 numbers}

Me: Are you not paying attention?

Scammer: You said 4 numbers correct?

Me: I clearly said 5 digits...twice. Is there something wrong with your hearing?

Scammer: Please say your zip one more time.

Me: {I make up 5 totally different numbers this time}

Scammer: Thank you Sir, now which Electric Company provides you service.

Me: What does your list say?

Scammer: {mentions 3 companies}

Me: None of those.

Scammer: What do you mean none of those?

Me: Again, something is wrong with your hearing.

Scammer: Sir, you are not being very cooperative.

Me: What gave it away?

{and they hung up}

Note: Your actual electric or gas service provider will never call you to apologize or offer you a discount. These calls are scams. So if you feel a bit snarky and you want to waste their time, give it a go and see how long you can keep them busy.

Lose My Email

If you start your email off like this guy saying you found me on LinkedIn the chances of you getting a scathing reply from me are pretty darn good.

Hi Rob,
I came across your profile on LinkedIn and wanted to see if you are responsible for the recruiting/talent acquisition efforts. I'm a Stanford Engineering grad and also an awesome recruiter with about a decade of experience. I have helped to place over 200 professionals across multiple industries including software engineers, engineering managers, designers, salespeople, product managers, and executives. I have many connections across the US. Is there anything I might be able to help your team out with recruiting for? If so, does 11:30am, 12pm and 12:30pm PST on Wednesday, Thursday or Friday work for a phone call to discuss? If not, I'd appreciate it if you could connect me with the right person. I look forward to hearing from you soon. Cheers,
Paul C.

My reply:

Hi Paul,
Well lah-de-da.

~Rob

P.S. Stop scraping people's emails from LinkedIn.

P.P.S. I don't care how many connections you have or how awesome you think you might be, the fact that you scraped my email from LinkedIn is enough to never ever refer you to anyone I know.

Paul replies... "My apologies I didn't mean to trigger you, I will remove your email right away."

Chapter 11

GoDaddy's Finest

"These are the best of the best of the best of the best."

Eric From GoDaddy

Hi this is Eric at GoDaddy...

I was reviewing your domains and was calling to see if they are still relevant to what you do.

Me: Yes they are!

Eric: Okay, may I ask what you do?

Me: You can, but I don't see how that is relevant.

Eric: Well sir, you have a considerable amount of domains.

Me: Yes, yes I do.

Eric: Well, we want to make sure you are using them properly.

Me: Seriously?

Eric: We want to help you maximize your experience.

Me: Okay, here's how you can help...stop calling people with lots of domains, we evidently know how to use them.

Eric: Sir...

Me: (click)

Thirty seconds later the phone rings...it's GoDaddy again. I didn't answer. They left a message saying we must've been disconnected and I should call them back.

Note: GoDaddy advertises they have millions of customers, yet weirdly I seem to be getting all their calls.

Chantelle from GoDaddy

My phone rings...

Caller: Is this Rob?

Me: Depends, who's calling?

Caller: This is Chantelle from GoDaddy

Me: Okay

Chantelle From GoDaddy: How is your day?

Me: What do you want?

Chantelle From GoDaddy: Well, we just want to look over your account and make sure everything is okay.

Me: Why? Is something amiss?

Chantelle From GoDaddy: Is something what?

Me: You know...off, not right, wonky, jacked up, messed up, not working.

Chantelle From GoDaddy: How is the traffic to your site, are you keeping busy, how can we...

Me: This conversation is boring...adios!
(click)

Note: I think the only reason I answer the phone anymore is to entertain people with my impressive phone skills that are reading my books.

Gary From GoDaddy

Phone rings…caller ID displays "GoDaddy".
{trying to resist the urge to pick up the phone as I know what they will ask me…crap, my hand clicked accept…and so here I go.}

Me: Hello

Gary: Is this Rob?

Me: None other, how can I help you?

Gary: This is Gary at GoDaddy.

Me: Gary you say? The Gary I heard so much about? The Gary who single handedly saved GoDaddy by calling thousands of accounts to talk to them about upgrading.

Gary: Hmm…uh…no I'm a different Gary.

Me: So are you the Gary that has the office in the sublevel basement who is only allowed to call clients when the others have failed?

Gary: No, not that Gary either.

Me: Well, you seem to be just an ordinary Gary then. Someone who got hired to do call checks on clients who eagerly await getting call checks from GoDaddy.

Gary: So you're okay with the service then?

Me: How much time do you have? I made a list.
{Gary hung up}

Note: You would think with all the times GoDaddy calls they would actually take the time to review my list.

Chapter 12

To Heck And Back

*"It's not the destination, it's the journey…
especially when you are on fire and screaming at everyone."*

Rob Anspach

Why Would You Invite Me To Your House

On Saturday my wife and I were at the grocery store. We didn't have masks on.

As the store no longer enforces that policy.

However we were among the minority who weren't wearing masks. Well at the checkout aisle the cashier was pleasant, and talked to us like normal people. Which was nice. As I'm paying for my groceries I see a woman exit the aisle she was in and as she passed by my aisle she gave me a dirty look. I just smiled back.

A few minutes later my wife and I were walking our groceries to the car and the same woman who gave me a dirty look drives up to us and says, *"I hope you're proud of yourself."*

I really had no clue what she was talking about but I answered...
Why yes, yes I am.

To which she retorts... *You think you're so special don't you?*

Me: Yup.

Her: You think you're so superior you don't need to follow the rules.

Me: Okay I'll play your game, sure.

Her: You're getting everyone sick by not wearing a mask, I hope you go to hell!

Me: Why would you invite me to your house?

{She flipped me the finger and sped off}

Note: Pfft…it's not even safe to go grocery shopping anymore.

How May We Irritate You

Sunday evening around 9:35pm...
I go to a website to get more information...
I see lots of options...
I click on the button to learn more about Option B...
I fill out the form to get even more information sent to me...
Five minutes later my phone rings...
It's late, I don't feel like answering...
I let it go to voicemail...
It was a rep from the website I was just on...

Then I get an email from the same rep...
"Thanks for your inquiry, I will be glad to help you with your selection."

Replying back I say: Can you send more information and exact sizes?

Rep: Sure, what options were you looking at?

Me: Doesn't your system show you that?

Rep: No, was it Option A, if so that's a good choice.

Me: What? No, it was not Option A. Why did I even fill out a form if it's not going to give you the right information?

Rep: Was is Option C?

Me: Holy crap...go away...I'm done with your company.

Rep: Sir, you filled out the form, so we are trying to help you with your selection.

Me: I don't care anymore...your system is flawed. You already irritated me and I don't care what deals you have, there is no way in hell I'm buying from you or your company.
Rep: Shall I have someone call you tomorrow?

Me: Remove all my information from your system and don't ever email or call me again.

Rep: Okay Sir, we'll have someone mail you the information then.

Me: Stop emailing me. Don't call me or mail me. Get rid of my information. I don't want you bugging me ever again.

{Monday morning around 7:55am...my phone rings...I let it go to Voicemail}

"*Hi Sir, we might have gotten off on a bad start last night, allow me to review everything with you today at a more convenient time.*"

{Five minutes later...get an email from this person}

Grr!

Note: I doubt even filing a restraining order would stop these companies from irritating me.

Chapter 13

You're In The Book Now

"And forever you will be…think of it as your legacy."

I'll Sue You

Hey Rob, you wrote 3 books about your dealings with people who call you. So why aren't you taking my calls?

{message I received through Facebook}

Me: I knew it was you.

Them: What?

Me: Have you heard about caller ID?

Them: Sure, but it's not about caller ID.

Me: Yes it is.

Them: No it's about you avoiding my calls.

Me: And that wouldn't be possible without a caller ID.

Them: But you take random calls from time wasters and scammers.

Me: Yes, because I have a caller ID that tells me who they are.

Them: The point is you would rather take a call from a scammer than from me.

Me: Yes that's the point.

Them: Why?

Me: Because their stories help sell books.

Them: My story could too.

Me: Are you a scammer or a time waster?

Them: Neither.

Me: Well, I think you are one or the other, which one is up to you.

Them: F- You

Me: Time waster it is then. Congrats you just made it into the next book.

Them: I don't want to be in your next book.

Me: I think that's too late now. You're in it.

Them: Take me out, I don't want to be in it.

Me: Well you should have thought about that when you sent me your initial message.

Them: I'll sue you.

Me: If you must.

Them: Take me out of your damn book now.

Me: Too late, you are so in it.

Them: I've had it with you. I've warned you. I asked you to not include me in your book. I'm done. You will hear from my lawyer.

Me: Okay I'll be waiting. But you're still in the book and I'm never taking your calls.

Them: F-You and good riddance.
{he blocked me}

I wonder how long it will take for his lawyer to contact me?

Should I wait anxiously by the phone?

Should I be worried?

Do you think I really care?

Oh, maybe it will provide more content for a future book.

Congrats You're In The Book

Four months after my company produced our 28th book...I received a Facebook chat message:

Them: Hey man congrats on your book.

Me: Which one?

Them: What do you mean which one, how many are there?

Me: So far 28 with 4 more in the pipeline.

Them: Wow, sounds like you don't need my congratulations then.

Me: Well I'd appreciate it if you bought one.

Them: Are they on Audible? I really don't have time to read?

Me: Let me ask you, do you binge watch Netflix programs?

Them: Yes, all the time.

Me: Great then you have time to read.

Them: I told you I don't have time to read.

Me: If you have time to binge, you have time to read.

Them: Look dude, I don't have time.

Me: If you have time to argue with people over chat, you have plenty of time to read.

Them: F-You.

Me: Is that a question or a statement? Because in my Rob Versus books when someone says F-You to me they usually get a spot in a future book.

Them: Go away.

Me: You initiated this chat. So you go away.

Them: F-off

Me: So you're saying you want a spot in my next book?

Them: I didn't say that, but you can shove those books up your a-hole.

Me: Congrats.

Them: For what?

Me: You made it in the next book.

Them: F-You
{and I got blocked}

Note: Not even sure I need to put a note here – the whole communication sort of tells you all you need to know about how to deal with me when sending me a chat. But ya know…someone will test me and then wonder why they are appearing in a future book.

The Price is Normal, You are Not

Hey Rob, I've been ripped off by several SEO companies and you came highly recommended.

Me: To help you or rip you off?

Them: I need your help.

Me: Okay

Them: I've spent thousands with nothing to show for it.

Me: Okay

Them: Well I need everything fixed so I can finally make money.

Me: So you don't have money?

Them: I have some but would like to pay you after I get results.

Me: So what I'm hearing is you've been ripped off a few times, you don't have money and want to pay me after I get results for you.

Them: Yes

Me: So you want me to spend dozens possibly hundreds of hours fixing stuff your other SEO people screwed up and then hoping you will pay me?

Them: Yes.

Me: No, that's not how I work.

Them: Well I was ripped off before and I don't trust people.

Me: But it sounds like you have no problem ripping me off if I don't do a good job.

Them: That's not what I said. Regardless, can you give me a quote?

Me: {gives quote}

Them: WTF that's high

Me: No that's normal, you are just used to selecting people who don't charge enough then when they can't deliver you say they ripped you off.

Them: So with your high quote are you going to rip me off right from the start?

Me: No.

Them: You're not going to rip me off?

Me: No, I'm not going to take you on as a client.

Them: What? I just explained to you my problem.

Me: Well I'll send you an invoice for $400 then.

Them: What? Why?

Me: Because listening to people's problems cost extra.

Them: You're an asshole.

Me: That'll be $400 more.

Them: Why?

Me: Because you don't respect people or their time or experience.

Them: F-You

Me: And you just said the magic word that gets you a mention in my next book.

Them: Book? Well I expect royalties.

Me: Not when you owe me $800

Them: I'm not paying that.

Me: Just like you were never going to pay me for my services either.

{and he hung up}

Note: I've been an entrepreneur for over 25 years and I've heard all the excuses and sob stories, and I know when a person isn't being forthright. Every time I allowed myself to be drawn into their drama and feel sorry for them, I got burned. So if they want to think I'm being an a-hole for telling them I don't want to work with them, so be it. Frankly, being called names is so much better than dealing with their hassles if they became a client.

He Went From Clubhouse Into A Book

Hey Rob why aren't you on Clubhouse?

Me: Well let me ask you, how much time did you devote in January to being on and learning from others on Clubhouse?

Them: In total?

Me: Yeah, how many hours?

Them: Roughly 15-16 hours a week so about 60 hours total.

Me: Did you make any money?

Them: Not yet, but it's a great place to learn and listen to others talk about making money.

Me: Well in the same time frame you spent not making money and just listening to others drone on...I produced 2 client books and just started on a third one.

Them: You don't understand, people are making money on Clubhouse.

Me: Yes, but you haven't.

Them: But I could.

Me: Doubt it. Why didn't you devote those 60 hours to working on your own marketing and pumping up your sales in January instead of listening to Clubhouse?

Them: I didn't make much money in January.

Me: Yeah, because you wasted your time on Clubhouse.

Them: You don't understand, Clubhouse is where all the gurus are hanging out.

Me: Oh, I understand...it's where you focus your energy. Look I get it... you are looking for answers, a magic bullet, a quick fix to help you solve all your problems and to make your business profitable. But without action, all the ideas, all the listening to others and the excitement of being in rooms with gurus isn't going to make your business better. Reduce the amount of time on Clubhouse and put more time into creating marketing for your business.

Them: If I reduce my time on Clubhouse I might miss out on the big idea that makes me a million dollars or more.

Me: And continuing to listen will prevent you from ever making any money.

Them: Well I guess you have life all figured out.

Me: I haven't figured out everything. I haven't figured out why I'm a magnet for these conversations...but I have learned to use these conversations to educate, entertain and engage my audiences. And now you're part of a future book.

Them: What?

Me: Yup, see what I did there. You are now part of a teaching moment for others to learn from.

Them: Huh?

Me: Never mind, go back to Clubhouse.

Them: This was a waste of time.

Me: If you say so.

{I was waiting to get unfriended or blocked...evidently he was too distracted by Clubhouse to do so}

Final Note: {As explained by Adam Hommey and Steve Gamlin}

Adam: I see a lot of people using Clubhouse unintentionally (meaning, with no plan).
The clue is if they are in there 14 hours a day, just listening.
The best way I know how to describe those who fail at Clubhouse vs. those who excel at it -- it's like the difference between signing up for 10 webinars per day and watching all of them, vs. hosting your own webinar and presenting it to an audience of good-fit prospects.
Oh, and here's the "big idea" that's "worth a million dollars" that any "guru" is going to share, on ANY platform, for free.
Ready?
"Put in the work. The harder you work, the luckier you'll get."
There, look, I found it for ya.
If you want the "how", open your wallet.

Steve: Is this one of those people who keeps 'hanging out where the gurus are'...but not 'doing' anything? The gurus have been on vinyl, cassette, VHS tape, CDs, DVDs, etc.
Every single one of those mediums *can* work...if you DO THE WORK.
Simply gathering in a new place or platform every time one launches doesn't do much for you.
It's like going from event to event, where all dynamic people are...yet sitting in the back nodding your head, saying "YEAH!"...but not applying the knowledge and growing your business.

You can learn more about Adam and Steve below...

Adam Hommey – https://www.ScheduleWithAdam.com
https://www.TheReachSystem.com

Steve Gamlin - https://www.MotivationalFirewood.com

About The Author

Rob is affectionately known as "Mr. Sarcasm" to his friends - to everyone else he's a Certified Digital Marketing Strategist, a Foremost Expert On Specialized SEO, a Serial Author, Podcaster, Speaker and Authority Broadcaster who can help amplify YOU to your audience.

Rob has also produced books for many clients including lawyers, doctors, copywriters, speakers and consultants.

Rob helps companies across the globe generate new revenue and capture online business. And he hates scammers with a passion.

Rob is available to share talks and give interviews.

To learn more about Rob visit **AnspachMedia.com** or call Anspach Media at **(412)267-7224** today.

About The Editors

Okay not really editors, more like sarcasm checkers. These are people who for some unknown reason really just wanted to be part of what I was doing and lend a hand to help me make this book super special. In return I promised them the world. Okay not the world. But I did grant them space below to share a little bit about themselves. So please visit them and tell them how much you really like me, and that I'm the most sarcastic person you know…I mean really let them know that this book changed your life in some way.

Parthiv Shah – is the Founder and President of eLaunchers.com. Over 300 dentists, physicians and other clients from all over the globe have benefited from working with Parthiv and eLaunchers.com. He is the author of his International Best Selling book, "Business Kamasutra", and is a contributor or co-author to six additional books. He is routinely invited to speak as technology expert at direct marketing conferences and small group mastermind sessions. Parthiv received his MBA in 1994. He has worked on over 10000 direct mail marketing projects and mailed over a billion pieces of direct mail. He is a veteran of the Indian Air Force, member of the Lions Club, a Leadership Montgomery Core Program graduate (class of 2016) and the proud dad of an Eagle Scout.

Ashley Armstrong – known as The Hidden Rules Expert, Ashley helps women in eCommerce gain clarity through her Mastermind. She's been featured in Entrepreneur, The List TV, CBS, NBC, ABC, FOX www.TheHiddenRulesExpert.com

Amy Tiemeyer - Volunteeraholic, Veteran, Military Spouse, and Story Teller. My superpower and passion is to help others, organizations, and groups do things that support and develop a better society. I have been doing this work for over 30 years and I have volunteered, coordinated, and contributed on every level of organizations supporting youth, fitness, military, veterans, and the arts.

Faith Sage – In 2014, Faith stepped away from the job of her dreams as the head pastry chef for a well-established country club to pursue copywriting. Only to learn long form sales copy wasn't her jam but websites, funnels and landing pages were. Today she blends the two - copy and funnels - and writes all about it in her daily emails. To find more titillating info on Faith head on over to her website and snag a FREE copy of her $97 per month print newsletter "The Funnel Manifest" but only if you say please... www.faithsage.net

Scott Paton – has been podcasting since the spring of 2005. He has executive produced and/or co-hosted over 45 podcasts. An internationally renowned speaker, Scott has presented to audiences on five continents. Thousands of entrepreneurs and NGO's have changed their public engagement strategies based on Scott's training. In late 2014, one of his clients inspired him to make a video course on Podcasting. After his course went live, Scott told his clients and many decided to make courses but needed help. He has become a co-producer with them His productions include all areas of life-long learning including Stock Option Trading, Alternative Health, EFT, and Relationships. Scott has over 496,500 students from 199 countries taking at least one of his 150+ courses. In 2015, Scott became location independent, spending most of his time in Europe, North Africa, Central and South America, with regular trips back to Canada to see his grandchildren.

Kristin Babik – is the Team Lead/Senior Loan Officer at Network Funding out of Houston TX. When not helping clients secure the perfect mortgage loan, she spends time teaching her daughter the important aspects of life, namely sarcasm. She loves meeting new people and networking with like-minded entrepreneurs. Kristin can be reached at https://nflp.com/loanofficer/kristinbabik/

Jaime McCormick – is a dynamic speaker who uses real life experiences to engage, challenge and serve his audience. His diverse expertise in mindset transformation is sought after, making him an international coach with clients in America and beyond. Jaime has been heard on I-heart radio as well as multiple pod-casts: Raw and Real, Fit World Live, Morning Gratitude, Bathrobe Moments, and Why Can't You..., to name a few. Jaime is empowering, inspiring and an authority on overcoming adversity. Jaime speaks on topics such as perception, power of forgiveness, cognitive restructuring and the power of words. He uses personal stories and examples of how a simple change of thought can start to shape a new future. He engages the audience by conversing with them, and not at them... thereby prompting them to get involved within the discussion. Also, he specializes in presentations that are clear, concise and easy to understand. He does not sell a "get rich quick" formula, inasmuch as he presents a raw and concise concept of how to achieve a full and rewarding life.

Emily Letran – is a serial entrepreneur, CEO of multiple dental practices, and private coach to many professionals. As an international speaker, she has been on TEDx and shared stages with countless business leaders including Sharon Lechter, Dan Clark, Dr. Howard Farran, and Linda Miles. She has been featured; Dental Town, Global Woman, See Beyond, Yahoo! Finance, Forbes, USA Today, and FOX. She is a contributing writer for Dental IQ, DrBicuspid.com, and Dentistry Today. Dr. Letran is the Founder of Exceptional Leverage Inc., host of ACTION To WIN seminars, author of several books, and Certified Kolbe Consultant helping teams grow with customized insights to boost performance. She can be reached regarding interest speaking, guest expert appearance, high performance coaching, consulting and marketing strategist by email at emily@exceptionalleverage.com or by visiting Emily at www.AmericanDreamCoach.com

Resources

THE INTERVIEW SERIES FOR ENTREPRENEURS

Rob Anspach interviews talented entrepreneurs who demonstrate an eagerness to share their experiences, their knowledge and their stories to help others succeed.

Listen to the Rob Anspach's E-Heroes Podcast today.

Available on:

Apple, Google, Himalaya, Stitcher, Spotify, TuneIn

Or

www.AnspachMedia.com

Rob Versus The Scammers

Protecting The World Against Fraud, Nuisance Calls & Downright Phony Scams.

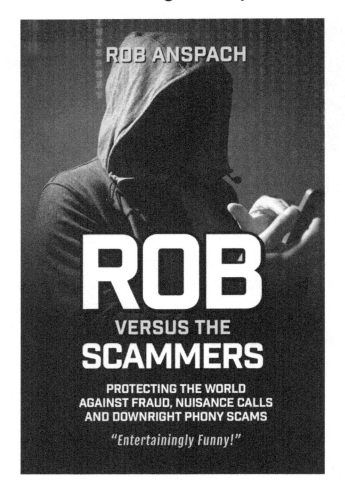

**Available on Amazon in Print & Kindle
or at…
www.RobVersusTheScammers.com**

Rob Versus The Morons

Overcoming Idiotic Customers With Wit, Sarcasm And A Take No Bullshit Attitude

**Available on Amazon in Print & Kindle or at…
www.RobVersusTheMorons.com**

Rob Versus Humanity

The Last Line Of Defense In Outwitting, Outlasting and Outliving Time Wasters, Fraudsters And Fools.

**Available on Amazon in Print & Kindle or at…
www.RobVersusHumanity.com**

Other Books By Rob Anspach

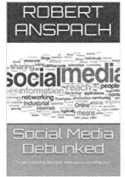  

Available on Amazon in Print & Kindle.

www.amazon.com/author/robertanspach

Books Produced By
Anspach Media
That You Might Enjoy

To learn more visit https://AnspachMedia.com/books

And One For The Road

The auto warranty scammers called while I was driving...

I answered.

Then proceeded to waste their time.

I asked if the warranty covered the transient conductive isolated polymer coating on my vehicle.

They spent several minutes asking around the call center about my question.

The scammer finally replied... "Sir, are you wasting our time?"

I laughed so hard I almost wrecked.

Remember to…

Share This Book!

Share it with your friends!

Share it with your colleagues!

Share it with law enforcement!

Share it on social media.

Share it using this hashtag...

#RobVersusTheEntitled

Made in the USA
Middletown, DE
25 April 2021